Thank you for your interest in the U.S. Department of Homeland Security (DHS) Science and Technology Directorate's (S&T) Transition to Practice (TTP) Technology Guide. This technology guide marks the culmination of an extensive foraging effort to identify cybersecurity technologies developed at the Department of Energy's National Laboratories. We're excited to share these promising cybersecurity technologies with you.

Through the TTP Program, S&T is identifying innovative, federally funded cybersecurity research that addresses cybersecurity needs and helping to transition this research into the Homeland Security Enterprise through partnerships and commercialization. This guide represents an important step in that process as all of the technologies included in this guide are ready to be piloted in an operational environment or to be transitioned into a commercially available product. If you're interested in piloting, licensing, or commercializing one of the technologies, please note that the DHS S&T TTP program is funding test and evaluation activities to validate technology performance, capability claims, and interoperability; and red teaming to find, reduce, and eliminate potential vulnerabilities.

This technology guide is the first edition of what will be an annual publication. To help direct future publications please reflect on the cybersecurity capability gaps in your own organizations, and share your thoughts with the TTP Program Manager (ST.TTP@hq.dhs.gov). Your input will help us identify timely solutions and inform future research efforts.

Again, it's our pleasure to introduce you to the TTP program and these newly developed cybersecurity tools from the Department of Energy's National Laboratories.

Sincerely,

Douglas Maughan

Michael Pozmantier

DHS S&T Cyber Security Division
Director

DHS S&T Cyber Security Division
TTP Program Manager

```
} else {
    temp=y/x;
    ans=x*sqrt(1.0+temp
}
                temp=x/y;
                ans=y*sqrt(1.0+te
return ans;

fcomplex Csqrt(fcomplex z)
{
    fcomplex c;
    float w;
    if ((z.r == 0.0) && (z.i = 0.0))
        c.r=0.0;
        c.i=0.0;
    } else {
        w = sqrt((sqrt(z.r*z.i
        if (z.r >= 0.0){
            c.r=w;
            c.i=z.i/(2.0*w
        } else {
```

S&T Directorate Strategic Plan

Homeland Security
Science and Technology

DHS S&T Mission

Strengthen America's security and resiliency by providing knowledge products and innovative technology solutions for the Homeland Security Enterprise

Goal 1:

Rapidly develop and deliver knowledge, analyses, and innovative solutions that advance the mission of the Department

Objectives:

- Provide knowledge, technologies, and science-based solutions that are integrated into homeland security operations, employing 24-36 month innovation cycles from project inception through operational testing

- Strengthen relationships with DHS components to better understand and address their requirements

- Focus on high-priority needs, through rigorous project selection and regular review of the entire R&D portfolio

- Implement processes that strengthen project management, evaluation, and accountability within the Directorate

Goal 2:

Leverage technical expertise to assist DHS components' efforts to establish operational requirements, and select and acquire needed technologies

Objectives:

- Provide scientific and engineering advice and services to strengthen DHS acquisition processes

- Encourage the private sector (with a focus on small business engagement) to develop technologies relevant to the HSE

- Incent owners of critical infrastructure and key resources to adopt technologies that reduce vulnerabilities and increase resilience

http://www.dhs.gov/scienceandtechnology

Goal 3:

Strengthen the Homeland Security Enterprise and First Responders' capabilities to protect the homeland and respond to disasters

Objectives:

- Better understand the needs and requirements of First Responder communities, including those on the front line of border protection and transportation security

- Create high-impact technologies and knowledge products – such as standards and protocols – that facilitate the safety, effectiveness, and ease with which First Responders do their work

- Advance the interoperability of communications equipment for First Responders

- Increase First Responders' access to information on best practices and product performance standards

Goal 4:

Conduct, catalyze, and survey scientific discoveries and inventions relevant to existing and emerging homeland security challenges

Objectives:

- Ensure effective construction and utilization of S&T laboratories in support of homeland security missions

- Improve S&T's knowledge and use of relevant national and international research and facilities, with a focus on DOE National Labs and DoD efforts

- Leverage academia to address Homeland Security needs and nurture the future technical workforce of the HSE

- Collaborate with OSTP and other government agencies to develop the national policy and strategic plan for homeland security research and development

Goal 5:

Foster a culture of innovation and learning, in S&T and across DHS, that addresses challenges with scientific, analytic, and technical rigor

Objectives:

- Increase S&T and the Department's awareness of cutting edge research and technology developments pertinent to DHS missions

- Promote a culture of openness, continual learning, innovation, and collaboration within S&T Directorate and across DHS

- Internally promote synergies and eliminate programmatic redundancies by creating mechanisms and processes to increase information sharing

- Support the development of a high-performing technical workforce at DHS

- Streamline business processes to increase organizational efficiency and effectiveness

Department of Homeland Security (DHS)
Science and Technology (S&T)
Cyber Security Division (CSD)

Homeland
Security
Science and Technology

The Cyber Security Division (CSD) is a Key Component in the President's National Strategy

Threats on the Internet change fast and cyber security is one of the most challenging areas in which the Federal government must keep pace. Next-generation cyber security technologies are needed to enhance the security and resilience of the nation's current and future critical infrastructure and the Internet.

In the Department of Homeland Security (DHS) Science & Technology Directorate (S&T), the CSD enables and supports research, development, testing, evaluation, and transition for advanced technologies in cyber security and information assurance. This full lifecycle of activities evolved in response to the President's National Strategy to Secure Cyberspace and the Comprehensive National Cybersecurity Initiative (CNCI).

The CNCI establishes a multi-pronged approach the Federal government will take in identifying current and emerging cyber threats, shoring up current and future vulnerabilities in telecommunications and cyberspace,

and responding to or proactively stopping entities that wish to steal or manipulate protected data on secure Federal systems.

The S&T Cyber Security Division addresses these objectives by:

- Discovering new solutions for emerging cyber security threats to the nation's critical infrastructure;

- Driving security improvements to close critical weaknesses in today's technologies and emerging systems; and

- Delivering new, tested technologies to defend against cyber security threats and making them available to all sectors through technology transfer and other methods.

CSD Focuses on Critical Vulnerabilities in the Cyber Security Landscape

Internet Infrastructure Security—Developing security protocols for the existing Internet infrastructure (browsers and routers, essential to daily Internet operation) so that users are not redirected to unsafe websites or pathways by malicious actors.

Critical Infrastructure/Key Resources—Securing the information systems that control the country's energy infrastructure including the electrical grid, oil and gas refineries, and pipelines, to reduce vulnerabilities as legacy, standalone systems are networked and brought online.

National Research Infrastructure—Providing the infrastructure that enables development and testing of technologies to address cyber security issues including botnets, worm propagation and defense, and denial-of-service defenses that protect Internet websites against attack; providing a data repository to support the cyber security research community.

Leap-Ahead Technologies—Develop "leap-ahead" technologies that will achieve orders-of-magnitude improvements in cyber security. One of CNCI's goals is to achieve a reliable, resilient, and trustworthy digital infrastructure.

> Our vision is a cyberspace that supports a secure and resilient infrastructure, that enables innovation and prosperity, and that protects privacy and other civil liberties by design. It is one in which we can use cyberspace with confidence to advance our economic interests and maintain national security under all conditions.
>
> — Quadrennial Homeland Security Review, 2010

Cyber Security Education—Helping to foster adequate training and education programs critical to the nation's cyber security needs by providing opportunities for high school and college students to develop their skills and by giving them access to advanced education and exercises through team competitions.

Identity Management—Evaluating and developing proof-of-concept solutions, and conducting pilot experiments of identity and access control architectures and technologies, as well as data privacy protection technologies for the homeland security community.

Cyber Forensics—Developing new cyber forensic analysis tools and investigative techniques to help law enforcement officers and forensic examiners address cyber-related crimes.

Software Assurance—Developing tools, techniques, and environments to analyze software, address the presence of internal flaws and vulnerabilities in software, and improve software security associated with critical infrastructure (energy, transportation, telecommunications, banking and finance, and other sectors).

S&T: Preparing for Next-Generation Cyber Threats

In the coming years, several cyber security challenges must be addressed. The most critical of these include Enterprise-Level Metrics, Combating Insider Threats, Combating Malware and Botnets, Digital Provenance, Situational Understanding and Attack Attribution, and Usable Security.

Transition to Practice: Accelerating the pace of technology transition

Homeland Security
Science and Technology

Michael Pozmantier
Michael.Pozmantier@hq.dhs.gov

In 2011, the Networking and Information Technology Research and Development (NITRD) Program of the White House named ways the Federal Government can rapidly improve the security of the Nation's cyber infrastructure. From that list, one of the NITRD's top priorities is to accelerate the transition of cybersecurity research into widespread deployment and use via the marketplace. As one of the agencies designated to address this priority, the Department of Homeland Security (DHS) tasked the Science and Technology Directorate (S&T) Cyber Security Division (CSD) with creating the Transition to Practice (TTP) Program. This newly initiated Program aligns with objectives four (Coordinate and redirect research and development efforts) and nine (Define and develop enduring "leap-ahead" technology, strategies, and programs) of the Comprehensive National Cybersecurity Initiative (CNCI). The TTP Program builds on the S&T Directorate's process of funding projects through the full research and development life cycle: research, development, test and evaluation, pilots, and transition.

In accordance with NITRD's recommendations for accelerating technology transition, the TTP Program's goals are to: (1) identify mature technologies that address an existing or imminent cybersecurity gap in public or private systems that impact national security, (2) identify and fund necessary improvements identified during pilot programs and test and evaluation activities, and (3) introduce cybersecurity technology throughout the entire Homeland Security Enterprise through partnerships and commercialization.

The TTP Program is targeting technologies that are most likely to successfully transition to the commercial market within two years and that will have a notable impact on the cybersecurity of our Nation's networks or systems. This is an ambitious endeavor with enormous potential for positive impact. Additionally, the TTP Program will provide a connection point for cybersecurity researchers, the Federal Government, and the private sector and ensure technology transitions from the research lab to the Homeland Security Enterprise.

For further information about the TTP Program, please email us at ST.TTP@hq.dhs.gov.

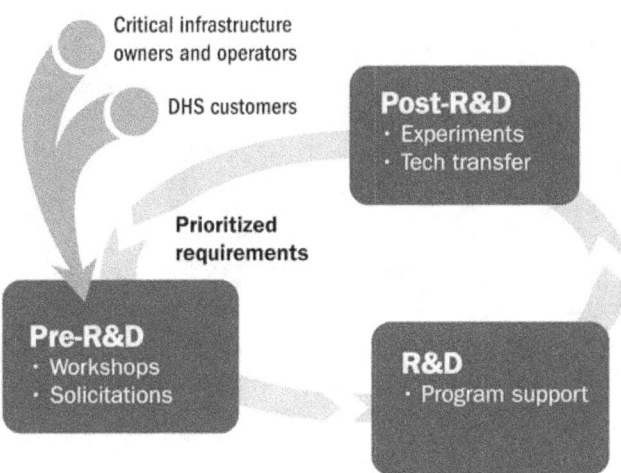

Cyber Security Division R&D Lifecycle

Code

Pro

ty

.010

0.0297 -0.1

nt Number

SSN

Hone: Producing insight by correlating machine and network activities

Glenn Fink
Glenn.Fink@pnnl.gov

Dan Best
Daniel.Best@pnnl.gov

Overview

HONE is a host-based cyber sensor that provides a new data source of correlated Host and Network data. Hone fixes a fundamental flaw in Internet protocol stacks to enable powerful insight for cyber defenders.

Customer Need

U.S. Government agencies and organizations are constantly experiencing a huge and growing number of cyber events in their networks. In 2011, DOE alone experienced 500,000 of them daily. For DOD the 2011 number was over 8,000,000 each day. Federal cyber systems need continuous monitoring, not just FISMA compliance. With all the host and network data from this monitoring, cyber defenders find it difficult to isolate root causes of break-ins because analysts cannot easily determine which processes are responsible for which communications.

Our Approach

Amazingly, a flaw designed into Internet protocols prevents analysts from correlating network communications to the processes that send and receive them. Network communication routing is kept separate from the routing of those communications among machine processes. *The unique contribution of the Host-Network sensor (HONE) is that it forms a bridge between the networking and processing parts of monitored machines that enables the sensor to know which programs are responsible for malicious network activities.*

The Hone sensor is installed in the kernel, the deepest part of the operating system, via a system patch and a small host-based agent that must be installed on each monitored machine. While this does imply managing the host-based agent, this cost is no higher than many existing solutions, and it enables us unprecedented visibility inside the machine from the network.

Benefits

The Hone sensors are freely available, open-source software. Wireshark additions are also freely available to view the data from the sensors. With Hone, defending analysts can characterize communication with 100% accuracy. Further, knowing the responsible program enables us to focus host-based tools on the many other important areas of each process's activities including open files, registry entries, libraries, and user information. Meantime, the performance impact of this sensor is small, comparable to common network data collection programs like tcpdump.

Competitive Advantage

Without Hone it is impossible to determine with certainty the process responsible for each communication. Analysts may rely on deep-packet inspection technologies to

DHS S&T Cyber Security Division
Transition to Practice Program
Technology Guide – Volume 1

Homeland
Security
Science and Technology

approximate the correlation, but these technologies can cost hundreds of thousands of dollars apiece, they can violate user privacy, and they can still just provide a guess about the process-packet correlation.

Connection-filtering, host-based firewalls are another alternative, but they only operate on the connection level, not every packet. This means that once you grant blanket permission for an application to access the network, you have no further control. Only Hone provides the precision to control communications at the packet level coupled with 100% certain attribution of responsible processes.

Finally, another kind of solution, multi-host management, uses host-based agents and provides monitoring services that rival Hone's in some ways, although none can give the absolute certainty that each packet goes to a specific process and no other as Hone can. These solutions are often quite expensive and include many management controls and visual tools in addition to simply monitoring packet-process correlation. Instead, Hone is simply a data source that can be taken advantage of by other security information management tools agencies already own. Additionally, Hone is open-source and freely available. We welcome collaborators and contributors to help us provide a growing feature set.

Next Steps

Hone is currently under development and we are seeking clients for pilot testing and further development. We plan to test Hone sensors as an operational prototype during FY13 and further develop higher-end monitoring capabilities. Our top priority is to provide the Linux and Windows 7 and 8 sensors in the open source at (https://github.com/HoneProject/). We also plan a MacOS X sensor and have a research prototype visualization for this data called, HoneViz, which may be available in the fourth quarter of FY13 or early FY14. We also welcome contributions to the open-source development effort.

What would you be able to do if you could rapidly isolate root causes of cyber break-ins seen on the network with absolute certainty that the process attribution is correct?

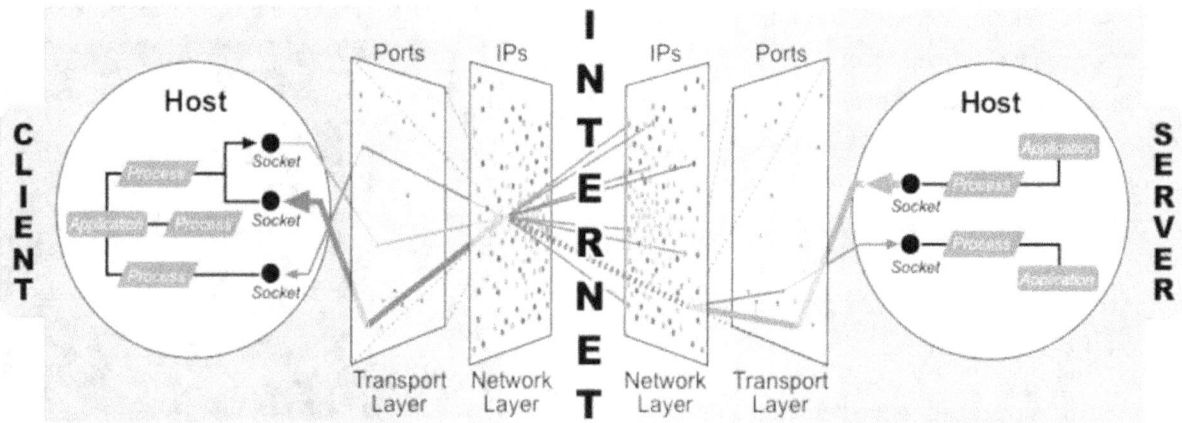

Hone provides correlated data that can enable an unprecedented end-to-end view of network communications.

CodeSeal: Tamper-proof Trust Anchors

Adrian Chavez
adrchav@sandia.gov

John Solis
jhsolis@sandia.gov

Overview

CodeSeal is a cryptographically secure obfuscation technology that provides tamper-proof trust anchors to protect commercial hardware and software from malicious tampering throughout their entire lifecycle.

Customer Need

The proliferation of counterfeit information technology (IT) products is a security threat often overlooked by government departments and infrastructure operators. In reality, high-end counterfeit products may already be providing backdoor access to secure and sensitive systems due to compromised government supply chains. A recent study by KPMG and the Alliance for Gray Market and Counterfeit Abatement (AGMA) estimates that one in ten IT products sold globally is counterfeit. How many IT products are currently operating in your organization?

Despite this bleak reality, critical software must execute securely and with high fidelity—especially within critical infrastructure systems. Because many components are vulnerable throughout a product's life cycle, we must assume that these systems are compromised before we receive them. Government IT departments need a cost-effective solution that can be retrofitted into these systems to provide key security properties, such as authenticity, confidentiality, and integrity.

Our Approach

Trust anchors are functional elements that can be introduced into information systems to provide unbiased measurement and unimpeded control capabilities. These elements provide verification that systems are functioning correctly and can serve as a foundation for additional, independent security services. To this end, Sandia National Laboratories (SNL) has developed CodeSeal, a cryptographically secure obfuscation technology that ensures trust anchors are tamper-proof and that an adversary cannot derive their function. Trust anchors serve to greatly reduce the risk of an adversary inserting malicious functionality into a protected system.

SNL's CodeSeal technology uses a customized compiler to obfuscate a software program, hiding the program's functionality from analysts and reverse engineers. The obfuscated code is executed with the aid of a trust anchor, which interprets the obfuscated code and ensures its integrity. Protecting this trust anchor is critical as it is the key to deriving the functionality of the obfuscated code. The obfuscated code can only execute when in communication with the trust anchor; it remains obfuscated when executing and at rest.

Benefits

CodeSeal's obfuscation routines are based on established and widely accepted cryptographic standards that are provably secure. This allows our technology to benefit users by satisfying several important security properties:

- Obfuscated code behaves as a true black box, assuming the trust anchor is properly protected
- The original algorithm experiences at most a polynomial time slowdown. Internal testing has shown a linear slowdown with a coefficient of two.

DHS S&T Cyber Security Division
Transition to Practice Program
Technology Guide – Volume 1

Homeland
Security
cience and Technology

- An adversary cannot be aware of what the device is measuring

- An adversary cannot understand or modify program functionality

- An adversary cannot subvert the system, as any modification will be immediately evident.

Competitive Advantage

Traditional software obfuscation tools typically operate on a source program by manipulating function and variable names or a program's control flow. Several public tools exist for a variety of languages, e.g., Proguard for Java. However, none are capable of preventing a dedicated, patient, and well-funded adversary from decompiling and reverse-engineering the obfuscated code.

Programs operating in critical government infrastructures using traditional software obfuscation are defenseless against a determined adversary.

SNL's CodeSeal technology is a promising solution that addresses the shortcomings of traditional obfuscation techniques:

- CodeSeal correctly assumes that an adversary is capable of analyzing complex systems

- CodeSeal is provably secure and cannot be reverse engineered.

Next Steps

Currently, CodeSeal is at a technology readiness level of 5-6 with several demonstrations prototyping the technology. It is ready to be piloted and tested within an operational environment to secure critical software from malicious tampering on potentially compromised systems.

Through laboratory testing, performance metrics can be gathered and the algorithm can be refined, if necessary. The algorithms within the CodeSeal technology have been designed so that they can be highly optimized through pipelining in hardware. A software implementation is currently available for demonstration, but performance can drastically improve with a hardware implementation.

Choreographer: A Moving Target System to Thwart Automated Network Attackers

Craig A. Shue
cshue@ornl.gov

Overview

Attackers regularly compromise the public-facing servers that organizations use to fulfill their missions. We regularly change the locations of these servers, disorienting attackers while still providing reliable connectivity for legitimate users.

Customer Need

Most organizations face ongoing and damaging attacks on their public-facing servers. At the same time, such servers are critical to the mission objectives of these organizations. Over time, attackers can scan organization servers and learn about the infrastructure and defenses, allowing the attackers to tailor their assault on our infrastructure. Each public server can became an attack vector and a foothold into an organization's network for adversaries. The cost of a security failure can be high. In 2011, the average cost of a data breach was estimated at $5.5 million. Other costs may be less quantifiable, including damage to the customer's reputation or even the customer's ability to complete its mission.

Our Approach

We frequently change the public addresses of protected servers, which 1) makes it challenging for attackers to guess the server's address, and 2) allows us to seamlessly redirect an attacker to monitoring infrastructure (called a "honey pot").

When contacted by a legitimate user—one without a prior history of attacks—the DNS server provides the correct address for the server and creates a network mapping to maintain the link.

This approach allows the DNS server to grant or deny access to legitimate users and seamlessly transition malicious users to honey pots upon detection. Organizations can use prior history to make decisions, protecting themselves based on past actions by a network.

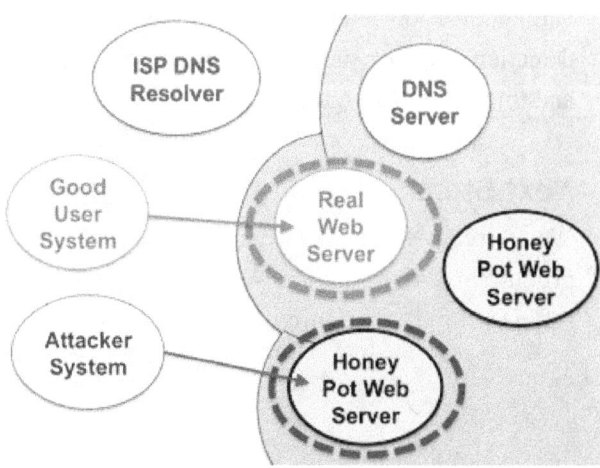

Benefits

- Our approach reduces attacker scanning effectiveness from around 100% to less than 1% for most network deployments.

- We can limit access to authorized requestors.

- We can study the diverted users, 95% of which are likely to be malicious users and parole the legitimate users.

- We enable policy decisions based on the source network, incentivizing ISPs to remove malicious clients from their networks.

- Deployment is straightforward and requires only minor changes in infrastructure.

- Performance overheads are minimal for smaller DNS zones and organizations can select which systems to place in protected zones.

DHS S&T Cyber Security Division
Transition to Practice Program
Technology Guide – Volume 1

Homeland
Security
Science and Technology

Competitive Advantage

While traditional firewalls can thwart access, they are based on signatures, and a single misconfiguration allows arbitrary attackers into the network. Dynamic and adaptive network approaches do not support migrating ongoing connections from the old address to the new one, causing connections to break. Our supports established connections even when addresses change. Our approach makes an explicit decision before the connection starts and during the connection, if needed. Unlike intrusion detection systems that rely on anomaly detection or attack signatures, our approach can detect and thwart zero-day attacks.

Next Steps

We are ready to begin early rollout in non-critical production environments. We are looking for partners interested in transitioning the technology.

USB-ARM: Architecture for USB-based Removable Media Protection

Logan Lamb
lamblm@ornl.gov

Overview

USB-ARM provides a simple, efficient, and customizable layer of security that brokers all communication between removable media and the operating system. USB-ARM guarantees that a set of user-defined criteria are met prior to allowing access to the removable media.

Customer Need

While the convenience of USB devices and removable media increase productivity, they also provide an effective attack vector for malicious software. Currently organizations have to compromise on their solutions for handling removable media and protecting against malware. Generally, organizations will either ban removable media use, resulting in lost productivity, or rely on a single anti-virus solution to eliminate infection. Unfortunately, no anti-virus tool has a 100% detection rate and many policies can be circumvented. The cost of such realities can be tremendous. The average cost of a cybersecurity incident totaled $214,000 in 2012, ballooning to $5.5 million if involving a data breach; it is only expected to increase as threats continue to evolve. Organizations require extensible tools to handle the evolving malware threat. With USB-ARM, an organization does not have to choose between technologies and can easily incorporate all enforcement tools into their removable media policy.

Our Approach

USB-ARM installs a driver that brokers all communication between the removable media and the operating system. Upon recognition from the operating system, USB-ARM blocks all communication to the device until a set of user-defined criteria are met. For example, a configuration might employ McAfee anti-virus, followed by AVG anti-virus, and finally an executable

detection engine. Access to the media is granted only if McAfee and AVG found nothing suspicious. Access to a given file is granted transparently if not flagged as an executable by the detection engine.

Benefits

USB-ARM guarantees that a set of user-defined criteria are met prior to allowing access to the removable media. USB-ARM eliminates any possible race conditions between security software and the execution of malware on removable media. Unlike current mechanisms, USB-ARM facilitates sequential use of multiple anti-virus engines, ensuring maximum protection. An organization can decide for itself what security properties are used to identify "clean" media. USB-ARM is simple, efficient, and transparent to the user. It is as effective as the sum of the user-defined stages, allowing customization to an organization's needs.

Competitive Advantage

USB-ARM prohibits access to removable media until all user-defined stages have been completed successfully. This capability allows organizations to easily tailor and extend their removable media policy. Currently, no other tool has this capability.

Next Steps

We are seeking partners interested in piloting and commercializing USB-ARM.

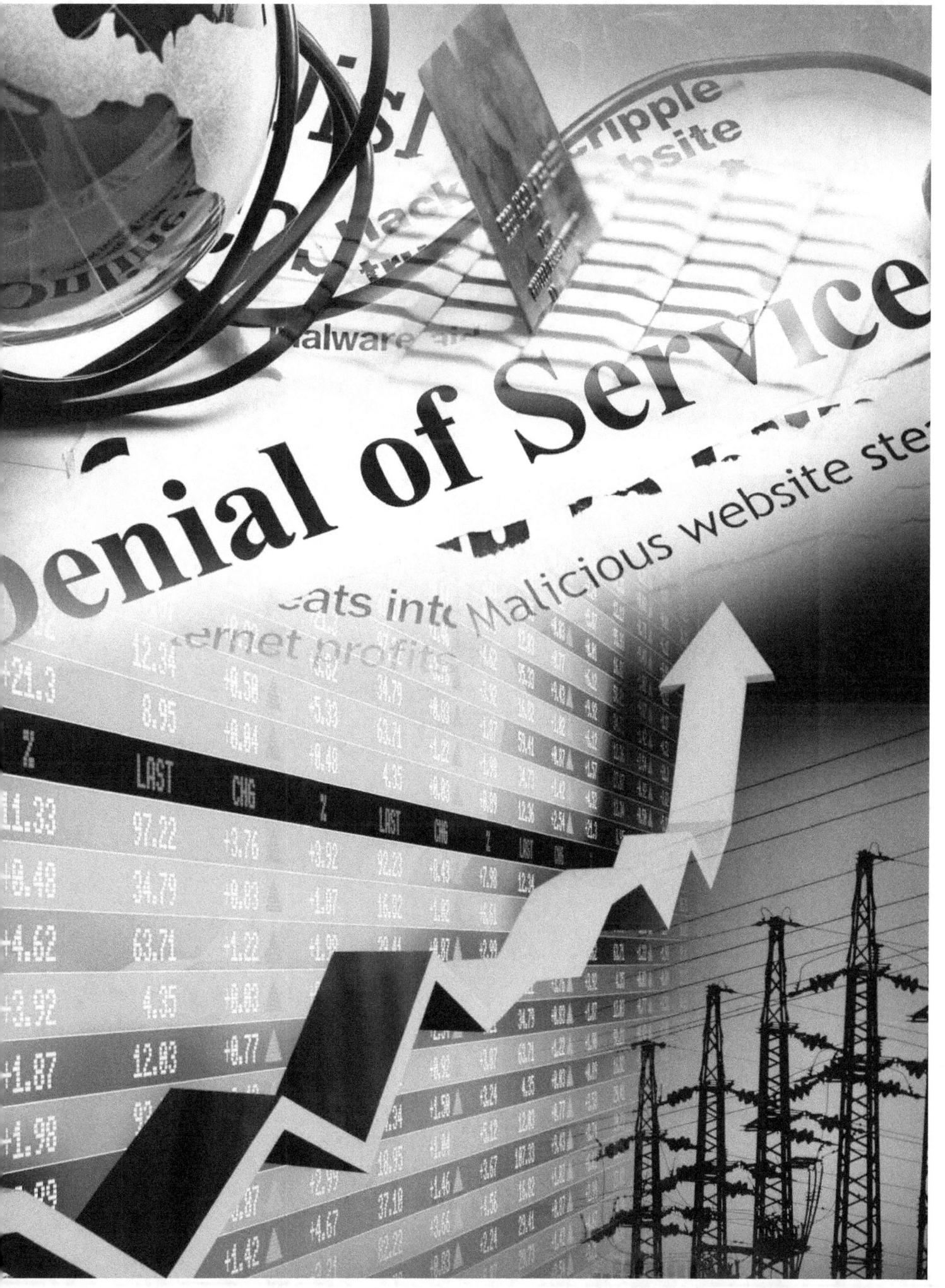

Hyperion: Detecting vulnerabilities and sleeper code, analyzing malware, and assuring software

Stacy Prowell
prowellsj@ornl.gov

Rick Linger
lingerr@ornl.gov

Overview

Hyperion is a new technology that computes the behavior of software, including malware, in all circumstances of use, without the need for source code. Hyperion operates on compiled binaries, rather than source code, to approach the ground truth of processor operations.

Customer Need

The first day a vulnerability is announced, a vendor loses, on average, $860 million in market value (Telang and Wattal 2007), and software security incidents cost an average of $300,000 (Aberdeen 2010).

There is a growing need for more complete analysis of software to account for all possible behavior, whether legitimate or malicious, without the uncertainties of approximations and heuristics. Such a capability will help assure newly developed and acquired software, reduce damage from vulnerabilities, and assist in analyzing malware.

Our Approach

For any critical software functionality, the Hyperion system generates associated program behaviors and the complete set of conditions under which they occur. These behaviors can be automatically checked for known malicious signatures and inspected by domain experts to assure correct operation and the absence of malicious content.

The key is Oak Ridge National Laboratory's (ORNL) Function Extraction (FX) technology that directly computes the behavior of software binaries, no matter how they were originally coded. FX transforms programs into procedure-free, "as-built" specifications based on deep semantic analysis that enables new kinds of reasoning. ORNL is the sole provider of FX, leveraging its institutional expertise in big data and High Performance Computing to address scale up and performance. Hyperion applies the mathematics of denotational semantics to transform input code into a functional representation, transform it into a structured form, compute its behavior, and abstract that behavior according to Behavior Specification Units provided by domain experts.

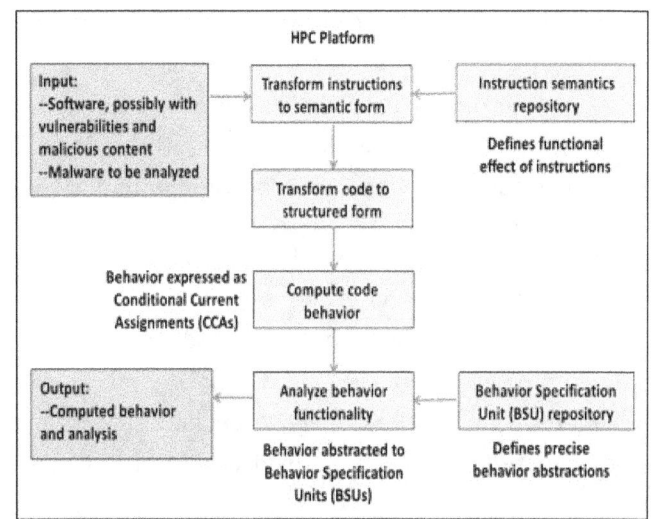

Benefits

Hyperion provides a repeatable, cost-effective means to achieve assured software. It permits validation with high confidence of the security of software for the deployment environment. It also permits discovery of the functionality of malware, even malware that is obfuscated and hidden. Because Hyperion coalesces and aggregates related behavior, malware that is distributed throughout legitimate code is revealed as just more

DHS S&T Cyber Security Division
Transition to Practice Program
Technology Guide – Volume 1

Homeland
Security
Science and Technology

cases of behavior. The technology has also been applied to polymorphic and metamorphic malware.

Competitive Advantage

Existing approaches to high-assurance software include testing, inspection, and scanning. Even the best testing can exercise only a small subset of possible executions, and inspections are time-consuming and subject to human fallibility. Scanning methods are largely syntax-based, depend on a priori signatures, and can be subverted by simple variations. Behavior computation used by Hyperion does not look for specific artifacts in code; rather, it computes all behavior, legitimate and malicious, to permit complete analysis and assurance.

Next Steps

ORNL is ready to customize, deploy, and support the Hyperion system as required by sponsors. Hyperion algorithms have been developed to execute in computing clusters that are readily available on the market for others to use. If necessary, these algorithms can be adapted for specific sponsor requirements.

The system is driven by definitions of the functional semantics of instructions. These semantics have been developed for a comprehensive subset of the Intel x86 instruction set and for the MSP430 processor. In addition, the system can apply semantic subject-matter abstractions of behavior provided by domain experts.

Beyond x86 and MSP430 code, the system is ready to be tailored for sponsor requirements for other instruction sets. Custom user interfaces can also be provided to integrate the technology with specific operational environments.

R. Telang and S. Wattal, "An Empirical Analysis of the Impact of Software Vulnerability Announcements on Firm Stock Price," IEEE Transactions on Software Engineering, 33(8): August 2007, pp: 544-557.

Aberdeen Group, "Securing Your Applications: Three Ways to Play," August 31, 2010, quoted in

http://blogs.aberdeen.com/it-security/quantifying-business-value-of-application-security-cost-avoidance-cost-savings/ (retrieved on 10/2/2012)

MLSTONES: The DNA of Cyber Security - An Organic Model for Identifying Cyber Events

Elena Peterson
elena@pnnl.gov

Overview

MLSTONES is a set of tools that support a methodology that can help you quickly find the needle (cyber event) in a haystack of data, even if you don't know which needle is there and the haystack is full of other types of needles you aren't interested in. MLSTONES can also help you identify new cyber events that are not already known.

Customer Need

Our reliance on cyber systems permeates virtually every aspect of national infrastructure. From banking, finance, and industry to agriculture and distribution, from national defense to power generation and delivery, software and the data it produces are the lifeblood for maintaining critical infrastructure, information, and the U.S. strategic advantage over our adversaries. The volume of data generated has outpaced our ability to effectively analyze it fast enough to prevent many forms of cyber attacks. In most cases, new forms of attacks cannot be detected with current methods. We need a method to drastically reduce the amount of data to be analyzed, to quickly characterize a cyber event, and to identify previously unseen types of attacks before they are executed.

Our Approach

We've translated several biology and bioinformatics concepts onto cyber defense data. Specifically, we've created a methodology that uses the concepts of protein identification and families, inheritance, and function to apply to a number of cyber-based data types. The MLSTONES process creates cyber "proteins" and then uses protein alignment techniques to generate families of proteins; it does so very quickly. With this method, we can then create a single representation of an entire family of entities, thus reducing the amount of data to analyze by several orders of magnitudes.

We can also infer the function of a "cyber protein" by its relationship to other similar proteins. This is the same process used in biology to discover similar proteins. This helps to identify completely new (zero-day) cyber threats.

```
>SERVER1
QLMAQMLQQANNNNNNNNQLMAQIIMQALQLMQATMGNIQINAQQQQMALQL
MALAWRWRWVWVVQTAGMMLLQAAQLMAMLQQAQLMLAAMLAMLATMAGQ
MLQMALATMAGQQQTAGMQQIQMALILQMQALALAWVWVVLAWRWRWVWVT
MAGQQWVVWMQLAQLMAQMALQTAGQMLQMALRAWWRWVWVVMLQQAQ
MLAMLQQANNNNNNNNQQMLQIAQMLIQAQMLAMQLAQTMG
>SERVER2
QMLQQAQLAMQMLQQAQLAMIIQQMLQAQQMLAMQQLAQTGMAMLAMLAM
QQLAQLAWVVQLAMMQQLATMAQTMAGQQTMAGGQAMLQIMLQANNNNNNNI
LALALALALALALALALANNNNNNNNNNNNNNNNNNNNLALALALALALALALALA
NNNNNNNNNNNNLALALALALALALALALNNNNNNNNNNNNNNNNNNNNN
NNNNNNNNNNNNNNNNNNNNNNNNNNNNLLLLLLLLLLLLLLLLLAAAAAAA
AAAAAAAAAAAAAAAAAALAMLQAQTMAGQLAM
>SERVER3
MLAMLANNNNNNNQMLAMLAQMLAMLAQQMLAMLATGMAMLAAMLAQQML
AAMLATGMALALLAALLAALLAALLAALLAALLAATGMAQQMATGMAMLALLAA
QLLAAMLAMLATGMAQLLAAQQTGMQQQLLAAMLATGMAQQTGMQQLALLA
ALLAALLALAAMLATGMAMLALLAALLAAMLAALLAAMLANNNNNNNVTGMANN
LLAAMLAMLAQLLAAMLAMLAAMAMLATGMA
```

Figure 1: An example of "cyber proteins"

For example, to analyze a very large catalog of software, the MLSTONES team has created a mapping of machine codes to the amino acids that comprise a "protein." We use this mapping and some scalable, parallel protein alignment tools to generate families of similar binaries and, finally, create a single representation (motif) for each family. We've now reduced the data to analyze a new binary by several orders of magnitude and can very quickly place a new binary into its family membership. Even a previously unseen piece of software can be characterized by its behavior at the machine level without analyzing or executing the code. We've found that our approach

DHS S&T Cyber Security Division
Transition to Practice Program
Technology Guide – Volume 1

Homeland
Security
Science and Technology

also works with many types of cyber data. We are currently researching new mappings for understanding malicious network activity and have analyzed text-based data, such as error logs and server behavior.

Benefits

The MLSTONES process can reduce extremely large data sets to much smaller sets of family motifs that enable identification or classification in near real-time. We can identify new objects of interest that are similar to known items and also identify completely new classes of objects. Our tools are customizable to the specifics of the data being characterized. With some research, completely new types of cyber data can be classified just by designing a new transformation function. While methods and tools similar to the MLSTONES approach have long been used in computational biology, none can match the speed of MLSTONES. Because MLSTONES can handle and process data in near real-time, we can apply it to the volumes and velocities of data found in cybersecurity applications.

Competitive Advantage

No other known technology uses this approach and obtains the same results as MLSTONES. There are specialized methods for analysis of other types of data, but none can support analytics on the scale required for cyber data. Generating signatures for cyber applications typically occurs in one of two ways—reactively or with expert knowledge. Reactive signatures are generated by reverse engineering their details and then building new rule sets or exact patterns for finding the same event in the future. Antivirus and network intrusion detection, for example, primarily operate in this mode and are plagued by the fact that they often cannot recognize new events that are highly related to prior events. On the other hand, expert knowledge signatures are obtained by asking subject matter experts to intuit what they believe are the most relevant attributes

to look for. While these are not constrained by the same limitations as reactive approaches, they can be heavily biased by the subject matter expert and may still be defeated by outside-the-box mutations on prior strategies. MLSTONES offers a third option that is guided, but not limited by prior events. MLSTONES can recognize similarities that are distantly related but still statistically significant. MLSTONES is also not biased by experts and can be used to **discover** relevant attributes from a large data set.

Next Steps

MLSTONES is currently under development for government clients. The general tools are being fully developed and tested at the Pacific Northwest National Laboratory. They're also being incorporated into a workflow engine and into a workbench environment. We are also in the process of researching the capability to identify malicious network activity in near real-time. We would like to put the tools into a pilot operational environment in order to fully test their capabilities and their scalability.

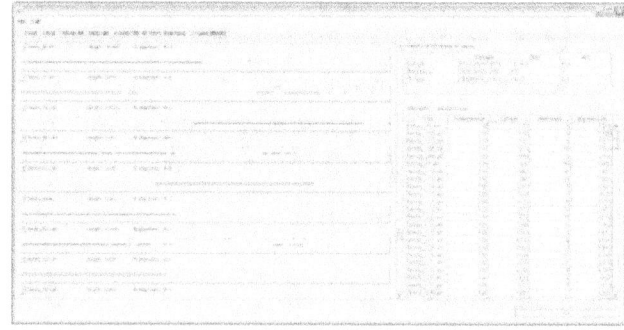

Figure 2: Visualization of family motif generation

Net_Mapper: Network Characterization and Discovery Tool

Celeste Matarazzo
Matarazzo1@llnl.gov

Domingo Colon
Colon3@llnl.gov

Overview

The Lawrence Livermore National Laboratory Net_Mapper is a software-based network characterization and discovery tool. Net_Mapper produces a comprehensive representation of IP-based computer network environments constructing visual representations of the targeted network based on observed behavior. The tool provides an iterative analysis platform from which network security managers and information technology (IT) personnel can explore the findings of each mapping operation.

Customer Need

Understanding the components, structure, and activities of a computer network is the first step in many cyber defense and cyber mission assurance operations. Mapping operations are needed to discover the network topology, including routers, switches, and end hosts as well as services running on these devices. The data is processed and stored to produce a map of the target network environment that may be viewed and analyzed by the appropriate IT and security personnel of the organization.

Our Approach

Net_Mapper applies a combination of active mapping, passive network traffic analysis, and host discovery techniques to accomplish the characterization of the network environment. Dedicated computer hardware is used to maintain performance and to provide a platform for follow-on analysis. Net_Mapper is also implemented as a "mapping appliance," a virtual machine containing an in-memory database-backed application for active mapping that can be placed behind firewalls,

on disconnected networks, or on other geographically or logically separated networks. The data from these mapping appliances can be combined out of band into a main mapping database for a complete network map without requiring special access. Data from all components is merged into a single data store for analysis and visualization.

Net_Mapper identifies and uncovers the network environment through a combination of:

- Discovering active devices
- Identifying communication paths
- Discovering open ports and associated services and applications
- Identifying active routing directives
- Discovering previously unknown devices
- Discovering unknown routing behaviors
- Identifying and processing transactions between hosts and users of the network
- Labeling content and resequencing network traffic

Benefits

Net_Mapper creates a queryable graph of any IP network with details of network entities, attributes, roles, and logical relationships. It can be utilized from outside a firewall or from any vantage point within a network, including multiple vantage points. The tool addresses the need for mapping IP networks to achieve network situational awareness without requiring extensive network preparation or prior knowledge and without compromising the security posture of the mapped environment. Net_Mapper has many controls

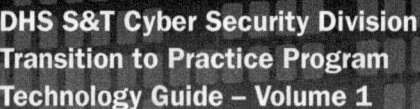

to enable the mapping operations to meet performance and security requirements. The system can be applied to government networks and commercial networks and can be used to generate a new map, corroborate or update existing maps, or fuse with additional types of data and information that may be available in the enterprise.

Competitive Advantage

Current tools for mapping networks are often slow and intrusive on network operations; they also require special exceptions to network security. The Net_ Mapper tool is designed and configurable to minimize disruptions and impacts on the target operational network and to require minimal intervention by network security staff. The tool uses well-established and tested network query tools and mechanisms while mapping. The system has a modular structure that allows the easy addition of new capabilities. For example, host-based sensors or asset information can be integrated into the system by adding the interface to the persistence layer with appropriate analysis and visualization primitives.

Next Steps

The Net_Mapper tool is currently available for pilot deployment for your network mapping and analysis needs.

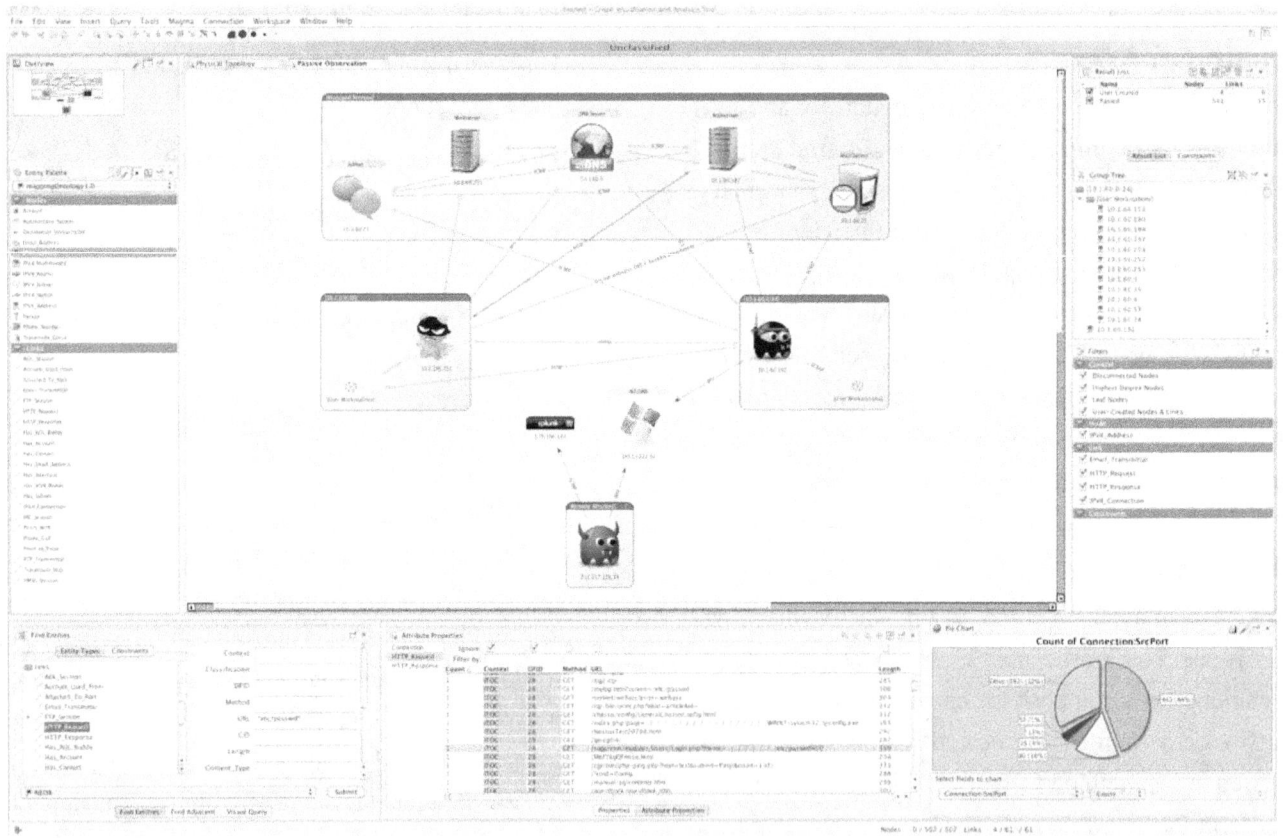

PathScan: Finding the Attacker Within

Joshua Neil
jneil@lanl.gov

Curtis Hash
chash@lanl.gov

Overview

PathScan quickly detects the movement of hackers once they are inside a computer network.

Customer Need

Hackers can and do penetrate perimeter defenses. For example, users clicking on phishing e-mails allow hackers to bypass firewalls and intrusion detection systems, providing a foothold in the network. Testing indicates click rates on phishing e-mails are as high as 10%. To get to the core network assets, hackers must traverse the network after this initial penetration. There is a need to quickly identify hackers once they have penetrated perimeter defenses, but before they can access core network assets.

Our Approach

PathScan targets the traversal behavior of hackers by building behavioral models to reflect normal activity, followed by passively monitoring network traffic and comparing it with the behavioral models. Our approach proceeds as follows:

- Build statistical models to characterize the network traffic between each pair of communicating computers.

- Break the network into millions of small paths.

- Passively monitor each path and test whether the data observed is likely to be normal according to the models built in Step 1 or, alternatively, it appears to be caused by a hacker moving along this path.

PathScan has two modes of operation.

- *Online:* Currently, PathScan is operational on LANL's unclassified network, analyzing millions of communications every minute.

- *Forensic:* PathScan can also be run in a forensic mode; it has proven effective in fleshing out attacks initially identified by security incident responders, discovering additional compromised machines that were undetected by the original investigators.

With a single commodity Symmetric Multi-Processing (SMP) machine, we are able to rapidly analyze LANL's 20,000 node unclassified network, examining the network in near real-time. We require network connectivity information in the form of DNS or NetFlow data. The output is a ranked list of the most anomalous hosts along with a heat map, as depicted in Figure 1.

Figure 1: Heat map of the detection of an actual Advanced Persistent Threat attack on LANL's network.

In Figure 1, dots are machines and lines are communications between machines. The color indicates the anomaly level. Trillions of objects were examined, the most anomalous of which, pictured here, contain the truly compromised machines as confirmed by forensic investigation. In addition, several machines identified

DHS S&T Cyber Security Division
Transition to Practice Program
Technology Guide – Volume 1

Homeland
Security
Science and Technology

in this plot were later determined to be compromised, yet the initial investigation missed these compromises, indicating the value of PathScan to aid forensic discovery of the attack.

Benefits

Detection is needed before attackers get to core assets. Early detection allows network operators the ability to shut down only those machines that are determined to be compromised, avoiding the shutdown of the entire network. This prevents the exfiltration of important data, but even more importantly, the difference between detecting an attack within the first few minutes and detecting the attack after several hours can be the difference between a minor security incident and an extremely costly attack. It has been shown that allowing an attacker to exist within a network for more than a few hours allows that attacker to penetrate the core machines, such as Active Directory servers. Compromise of these servers forces network operators to shut down the entire network, possibly for several weeks, in order to ensure effective removal of the compromise.

Competitive Advantage

Commercial products mostly look for exact signatures of previous attacks, whereas our methods are statistical in nature, allowing us to detect both known and zero-day behavior. Many government solutions only monitor data at the perimeter, while ours examines internal data, finding the attacker once they are inside. Finally, academic approaches generally do not scale well or are only applied to synthetic, non-realistic networks. PathScan, on the other hand, has scaled to very large networks, has scaled up to millions of computers, and has been validated on large operational networks.

Next Steps

We are actively developing PathScan. We seek partners to provide:

- *Pilots:* Live networks are needed for continued validation. Access to these networks will aid us in ironing out operational issues. In addition, any attacks identified on these networks will aid PathScan researchers in tuning the approach for future attack identification. These pilot network operators will be provided with analysis results and real-time protection using PathScan.

- *Commercialization:* The PathScan team at LANL is a research and development (R&D) organization, not a commercial software shop. We seek commercialization partners to provide software solutions that will encapsulate the PathScan technology in a commercial-grade software environment.

- *Research Funding:* While PathScan has proven effective in identifying Advanced Persistent Threat (APT) activity, research on improvements are ongoing. More advanced statistical models and better data collection mechanisms are important to stay ahead of the threat. We seek R&D funding to support the further improvement of PathScan.